Cendrillon

Cendrillon
A Cajun Cinderella

By Sheila Hébert Collins
Illustrated by Patrick Soper

PELICAN PUBLISHING COMPANY

Gretna 1998

*This book is dedicated with love and appreciation to
Carrie Lou and Don Collins, my mother-in-law and father-in-law.
Both teachers in New Orleans for more than thirty years, they encouraged
me to become a teacher as well as instilled in me a deep love for
New Orleans. They were both instrumental in getting me my first teaching
job in Algiers. With their encouragement, I was able to continue
teaching for twenty years and retire so that I could become an author.*

---

*The word "Pelican" and the depiction of a pelican are trademarks
of Pelican Publishing Company, Inc., and are registered
in the U.S. Patent and Trademark Office.*

Library of Congress Cataloging-in-Publication Data

Collins, Sheila Hébert.
    Cendrillon : a Cajun Cinderella / by Sheila Hébert Collins ;
illustrated by Patrick Soper.
       p.   cm.
    Summary: A Cajun variant of the Cinderella tale set in New Orleans
and including French words and phrases which are defined on the
bottom of each page.
    ISBN 1-56554-326-2 (hardcover : alk. paper)
    [1. Fairy tales. 2. Folklore—France.]   I. Soper, Patrick, ill.
II. Cinderella. English. III. Title.
PZ8.C6953Cg 1998
398.2'09444'02—dc21
[E]
                                                    98-19955
                                                       CIP
                                                         AC

French editing by Barbara H. Hébert

Printed in Hong Kong
Published by Pelican Publishing Company, Inc.
P.O. Box 3110, Gretna, Louisiana 70054-3110

Cendrillon

Once upon a time there lived a fine gentleman who had a beautiful home on St. Charles Avenue in New Orleans. He had one child, a daughter. She was *très belle!* He gave her all that he could buy and spoiled her terribly because she had no mother. The little girl did wish for a mother and her *père* knew this. So he married a woman with two daughters, hoping it would make his *petite fille* happy.

Cendrillon (Son-dree-ONH)—French for Cinderella
très belle (tray bel)—very pretty
père (pair)—father
petite fille (p'teet fee)—little girl

The new *belle-mère* had not been married one day when she became very jealous of her husband's child. She gave her stepdaughter all the hard and dirty work to do while her own daughters pampered themselves all day long. When her work was done, the *petite fille* rested by the fireplace among the cinders. From that day on, those mean stepsisters called her *Cendrillon*. But, *pauvre bête*, Cendrillon would not tell her *père* about any of this since he thought his new wife was so perfect.

belle-mère (bel mair)—stepmother
pauvre bête (poh-vruh bet)—poor thing

Mais, ça s'adonne, the fine gentleman died. His *grande maison* soon fell in disrepair and his widow had to sell it to buy a small, shabby shotgun house across the river.

mais (meh)—but
ça s'adonne (sa sa-DUN)—it so happens
grande maison (grahnd meh-ZONH)—big house

Cendrillon was given the dirty attic for her room and rags for clothes. But did she *boudez*? *Mais non!* She made friends with *les pigeons*, which would perch on the attic window every day. And she had lots of friends down by the levee: *le cocodrie, le canard, le crabe, le pigeon de mer, le pélican,* and, best of all, *les écrevisses.* She even made little clothes for her friends.

boudez (boo-DAY)—pout
mais non (meh nonh)—absolutely not
pigeons (pee-ZHONH)—pigeons
cocodrie (ko-ko-DREE)—alligator
canard (ka-NAHR)—duck
crabe (krahb)—crab
pigeon de mer (pee-ZHONH duh mair)—seagull
pélican (pay-lee-KAHNH)—pelican
écrevisses (ay-kruh-VEES)—crawfish

Her long days were filled with jobs to do for her *belle-mère* and ugly *belles-soeurs,* but Cendrillon always did her *ouvrage* and had time for *ses bons amis.*

belles-soeurs (bel suhr)—stepsisters
ouvrage (oo-VRAHJH)—work
ses bons amis (say bonh zah-MEE)—her good friends

Now across the river from Cendrillon's
home lived Alphonse Thibeaux and his son,
Ovey. Monsieur Thibeaux was one of the richest
men in the city. He decided it was time for
Ovey to marry.

Using his connections, he had Ovey named Rex,
king of Carnival. He would have the biggest Mardi Gras ball in
the city and invite every unmarried girl in New Orleans. The
invitations were sent out by carriage, horseback, and pirogue.

Alphonse (al-FONS)—a Cajun name
Thibeaux (tee-BO)—a Cajun family name
Ovey (oh-VAY)—a Cajun name
monsieur (m'SYUHR)—mister
Mardi Gras (mar-dee grah)—Fat Tuesday, a Louisiana celebra-
    tion before Lent
pirogue (pee-rohg)—a shallow cypress boat

In Cendrillon's home, the invitations were received with joy.

"*Mon Dieu*, we are all going to the Rex Mardi Gras Ball!" the sisters shouted.

"*Et moi?*" asked Cendrillon.

"*Oui, et toi!*" laughed *les belles-soeurs*.

"*Oui*," said *la belle-mère* with a wicked smile. "Of course you may go, *if* you finish your chores and *if* you have something to wear."

mon Dieu (mohnh dyu)—my heavens
et moi? (ay mwa)—and me?
oui, et toi (wee, ay twa)—yes, and you

Cendrillon worked hard all day and made red beans and rice for dinner. But when it was time for the ball and the carriage had arrived, her *belle-mère* said, "*Mais, ça c'est triste, Cendrillon.* You are not ready for the ball?"

"*Mais non, ma belle-mère,* I cannot go to the ball," answered Cendrillon sadly.

"Not going! *Ça c'est dommage! Au revoir, Cendrillon,*" cackled the mean *belles-soeurs.*

mais, ça c'est triste (meh, sa say treest)—well, that's sad
ça c'est dommage (sa say doh-MAHJH)—that's a shame
au revoir (oh ruh-VWAHR)—good-bye

Pauvre bête, Cendrillon went up to her attic room and sank sadly down on her moss bed, feeling *tout à fait mal. Tout d'un coup,* she heard a tapping at her window. It was Pierre, *le pigeon.*

He signaled her to go down by the levee. She ran down there and—*mais jamais*—her friends had not forgotten her. They had been very busy making her a beautiful party dress for the ball.

"Mon Dieu! Ça c'est beau! Merci, merci!" she cried. Cendrillon ran to the top of the levee and yelled at the carriage, *"Arrêtez! Arrêtez!"*

tout à fait mal (too tah fay mahl)—very bad
tout d'un coup (too duhnh koo)—all of a sudden
mais jamais (meh zhah-MEH)—well, good grief
ça c'est beau—(sa say bo)—it's very pretty
merci (mair-SEE)—thank you
arrêtez (ah-reh-TAY)—stop

She dressed quickly, then ran to the carriage and jumped in. Her *belles-soeurs* stared in surprise, then began grabbing at her and screaming, "Those are my beads! That's my ribbon! Those are my bows!" And before long, Cendrillon was in rags again and was pushed out of the carriage. She was left sitting there on the ground, in a cloud of dust.

La chère petite fille ran to the levee in tears and sank down. Soon she felt someone beside her. She looked up and saw a beautiful lady.

"*Bon soir, madame. Qui êtes vous?*" asked Cendrillon.

"I'm your fairy *marraine* and I've come to help you," the beautiful lady said. From the sky came a magic wand. "Now dry your tears. We have work to do before you go to the ball."

chère petite fille (sha p'teet fee)—darling little girl
bon soir (bonh swahr)—good evening
madame (ma-DAHM)—ma'am
qui êtes vous? (kee et voo)—who are you?
marraine (ma-REN)—godmother

"*Allons-y!*" said *la marraine* as she held her magic wand. "The first thing we need is a nice cushaw, *ma petite fille*. Go to the garden and find a good one. *Dépêche-toi!*" Cendrillon did not *comprend* but she obeyed.

"And now *le gris-gris!*" said *la marraine*. "Hot *boudin,* cold *coosh coosh.* Come on, magic—poosh, poosh, poosh!" And with that the cushaw turned into a beautiful carriage.

allons-y (al-ohnh ZEE)—let's go to it
cushaw (kuh-SHAH)—a type of squash
dépêche-toi (day-PESH twa)—hurry up
comprend (kohnh-PRAHNH)—understand
gris-gris (gree gree)—magic
boudin (boo-DANH)—Cajun sausage
coosh coosh (koosh koosh)—fried cornmeal served with milk and
    sugar

"What we need now are some fine big . . . *écrevisses!*" said *la marraine*. Cendrillon jumped up and ran over the levee for *ses amis,* the crawfish. She brought six of them to *la marraine*. Marraine touched them with her wand and said her magic words: "Hot *boudin,* cold *coosh coosh*. Come on, magic—poosh, poosh, poosh!" With that, the crawfish turned into beautiful red horses. Pierre, *le pigeon,* became a fine footman, and *le crabe* became a fat coachman.

"*Mais, quoi t'en crois?*" asked *la marraine*.

"*Très magnifique!*" Cendrillon cried.

"*Mais, allons,*" said *la marraine*.

"*Mais non. Regardez-moi!*" replied Cendrillon.

"*Mon Dieu! Ça c'est bête!*" said *la marraine*. With those words, she touched Cendrillon with her magic wand and—*voilà*—there stood Cendrillon in a beautiful Mardi Gras gown with a dainty mask to match and tiny mother-of-pearl *souliers* on her feet.

mais, quoi t'en crois? (meh, kwa tahnh krwa)—well, what do you
   think of it?

très magnifique (tray mah-nyee-FEEK)—magnificent

regardez-moi (ruh-gar-day mwa)—look at me

ça c'est bête (sa say bet)—that's foolish

voilà (vwah-LAH)—there

souliers (sool-YAY)—slippers

"*Ecoute, Cendrillon. Vas,* but don't forget—you must return by *minuit* and not an instant later, or all my *gris-gris* will vanish and you will become as you were before," warned *la marraine.* *"Bonne chance!"*

The carriage crossed the river on the ferry and rolled along Canal Street toward the Grand Ballroom in the Roosevelt Hotel.

écoute (ay-KOOT)—listen
vas (vah)—go
minuit (mee-NWEE)—midnight
bonne chance (bun shahns)—good luck

When Cendrillon's coach arrived, Rex saw the *très belle fille* and helped her up the steps. Then all the guests in the ballroom turned to look at the sight of Cendrillon and Rex.

très belle fille (tray bel fee)—very beautiful girl

The guests whispered, "Who is this *très jolie fille?*" Rex led her to the dance floor and before their first dance was over, he had fallen hopelessly *en amour*. They danced together all evening, in a world of their own.

très jolie fille (tray zho-lee fee)—very pretty girl
en amour (ahnh ah-MOOR)—in love

Cendrillon was startled by the chimes of *minuit* from St. Louis Cathedral. *Tout d'un coup,* she ran from the dance floor, down the large hallway, and to the ferry, with Rex at her heels, shouting, *"Viens ici! Quoi y a?"* As the chimes rang *douze,* everything became as it was before—all but Cendrillon's beautiful mother-of-pearl slippers.

viens ici! (vyanz ee-SEE)—come here!
quoi y a? (kwa ee ah)—what's wrong?
douze (dooz)—twelve

As Cendrillon jumped for the ferry, a slipper fell off her foot onto the dock. When Rex reached the dock, he saw that his beautiful queen was crossing the river on the ferry. He picked up her slipper and sadly walked back to the ball.

Cendrillon reached home out of breath and filled with sadness. All she had left of her magical night was one slipper made of mother-of-pearl. She slowly walked upstairs to her attic room. She placed her slipper under her moss mattress and went to sleep, dreaming of her *amour*, Rex.

De bon matin, les belles-soeurs were chattering away about the beautiful lady at the ball with whom Rex had fallen hopelessly *en amour.*

"*Et là!* How could she run off at *minuit* like that? *C'est fou!*" one of *les belles-soeurs* said. Cendrillon listened but never said one word.

de bon matin (duh bonh ma-TANH)—early in the morning
et là! (ay lah)—a Cajun expression meaning "well!"
c'est fou (say foo)—that's crazy

At that moment, there was a great trumpet fanfare at Gallier Hall. Crowds of people gathered. Ovey Thibeaux—Rex—stood before the people and held up the little slipper.

"This is the slipper of my queen. I will marry the *mademoiselle* whose foot will fit this slipper. My court will visit each and every home in this city." The search began *tout de suite*.

mademoiselle (mad-mwa-ZELL)—young lady
tout de suite (toot sweet)—right away

When Rex's court arrived at Cendrillon's little shotgun house, her *belles-soeurs* were eager to try to get their *gros* feet into that slipper. Cendrillon hid around the corner as her *belles-soeurs* argued about who would be first. Try as they would, they could never get the slipper to fit.

"May I try, *s'il vous plaît?*" Cendrillon asked.

"*Mais oui,*" said the man.

"*Comment ça s'fait?*" shouted *les belles-soeurs.* "She is Cendrillon—for sure not fit for Rex!"

gros (groh)—big
s'il vous plaît (seel voo play)—please
mais oui (meh wee)—of course
comment ça s'fait? (koh-MOHNH sa suh fay)—what for?

"We are ordered by Rex," the man answered as he placed the slipper on Cendrillon's foot. Cendrillon took the other slipper out of her pocket and put it on. With the magic shoes back on her feet, the *gris-gris* returned and Cendrillon changed into *la belle fille* everyone had seen with Rex.

"*Mon Dieu!*" screamed *les belles-soeurs* as they fell to their knees begging forgiveness from Cendrillon. Cendrillon told them she would forgive them and they could even come *faire la veillée*.

faire la veillée (faihr la vay-AY)—visit

Then the men of Rex's court hurried her off to St. Charles Avenue, where Ovey Thibeaux was anxiously waiting. Cendrillon told Ovey and his family the whole story. "Kee yah!" they all yelled out. Right then and there they all jumped on the streetcar and went straight to the French Quarter to get married at St. Louis Cathedral.

kee yah (kee yah)—a Cajun expression meaning "wow"

Cendrillon and her Rex moved into a mansion next to the Mississippi River, where Cendrillon could still have *ses petits amis*. And as they say in the Crescent City, *"Laissez les bons temps rouler!"* And they did.

C'est tout!

ses petits amis (say p'tee zah-MEE)—her little friends

laissez les bons temps rouler (less-AY lay bonh tonh roo-LAY)—
    let the good times roll

c'est tout (say too)—that's all

RED BEANS AND RICE

1 onion, minced
¼ cup vegetable oil
1 lb. beef, pork, or turkey smoked sausage, sliced
1 can Rotel or other spicy chopped tomatoes

2 cans light-red kidney beans
2 cans cream-style kidney beans (or 1 can refried beans and 1 can light-red kidney beans)

Sauté onion in oil over high heat. Add sausage and tomatoes. Simmer over low heat for 20 minutes. Add beans. Stir until blended and simmer 15 minutes. Serve over rice. Corn bread and salad make the meal complete. *Ça c'est bon!*

ça c'est bon (sa say bonh)—that's good